HOW TO TRAIN A PUPPY WITH A CLICKER

11 MOST COMMON PROBLEMS PEOPLE FACE WHEN THEY FIRST START TRAINING THEIR FURRY FRIEND WITH A CLICKER

BY SMITH R. LARKIN

TABLE OF CONTENTS

INTRODUCTION

Have you ever wondered what could be the easiest possible way to communicate with your furry friend? I certainly did. I didn't ask myself only that, but a lot more. Although making communication more pleasant was certainly a great goal, for me, it wasn't the only thing I cared about. I wanted more.

Abundance is what I was after, to be able not just to have a mediocre relationship with my pet, but instead have an excellent one. The main question, though, was: *How can I make everything more efficient, a lot faster, and more enjoyable?* Not only for me, but for my dog too.

After a while, I found out about clicker training and its benefits. But, to be honest, I was skeptical at first. I mean, why can't I just use my voice and mark the behavior I liked with a simple "Yes" or "Good boy/Good girl"? Why should I use a clicker? I had my doubts.

I began to study a lot more about the history of training with a clicker. Furthermore, I was curious about how this whole process worked and why a lot of people were talking about it. Was it true? Could it really make your training sessions more effective and more fun? I needed to know. Although I had my doubts, I didn't let that stop me. I had to study this concept, try it, and see for myself.

Now, I can look back and see why a lot of people, when they first hear about this concept, are exactly like I was in the beginning, suspicious. I can understand them a lot better and feel exactly as they do.

"Why use a clicker if, in the end, you will get rid of it and eventually just use your voice?"
"When should I stop using the clicker?"

"Do I have to use the clicker for the rest of my life?"

"Will my dog only perform when there is a clicker and a treat?"

"What should I use as a training treat?"

"Is it important to only use one type of clicker, or could I just use my voice, a pen, a mini stapler, snap my fingers, or just use my tongue to produce a unique sound?"

"Where can I buy a clicker that is perfect for my needs and won't cause my dog to be afraid of that loud sound?"

"How old should my puppy be before I start clicker training?"

"What do I do if I have more than one dog?"

"Is it possible to potty train a dog using a clicker?"

These were just a few of the questions I, and people who are just starting out on this journey, had to deal with. At first, everything looked a little bit overwhelming, kind of like it was too much. But now, the great news is that we have the answers.

Yes, it is possible to clicker train your dog and to make it fun and efficient at the same time. Yes, there is nothing that complicated about this technique, and everybody who has a puppy or an adult dog can start to use the same concepts this book provides. Here you will find everything you need to know about how you can use this tool to teach your dog new tricks and new behaviors, and not only teach them but make them as strong as they can be.

The bottom line: It doesn't matter if your pet is just a puppy or an adult, if you have never used a clicker, or if you are just a beginner. This book will show you what clicker training (training with a clicker) is, how it can benefit you, where most people get stuck, the common problems they face, and how to make sure you will never make those mistakes. Here you will find everything you need to know about how you can use this tool to teach your dog new tricks and new behaviors, and not only teach them but make them as strong as they can be.

WHAT CLICKER TRAINING IS

First of all, let's define what clicker training is, how clicker training works, how to "charge" this tool and a few other basics things.

WHAT CLICKER TRAINING IS

When people ask me what clicker training is, I like to answer back and just say that it is a way to tell your dog he tried something that worked. A click is neither a reward nor a command, it is just a marker we use for better communication with our furry friend. Training with a clicker is a method that uses a unique sound to tell your pet he has done something right and that a reward is coming. What makes a clicker so effective is its distinct sound, which is very hard to replicate in our daily life.

Although this tool is so effective because of its distinct sound, if you don't pair that noise with a treat (e.g., "What a great job. Goodie is on its way"), the clicker itself becomes meaningless. The great news, though, is that if you "load this tool" and give meaning to it, you can train a new behavior at the drop of a hat, and make the whole process a lot more fun and enjoyable.

IF A CLICK IS JUST A MARKER WHY NOT USING THE WORD "YES," "GOOD BOY/ GOOD GIRL

Because this is a frequently asked question, I decided to dedicate a whole chapter to it, but until we get there, I think we should talk about this right from the start.

If the clicker is just a marker, what should you be using — a verbal marker (i.e., "Good," "Yes") or this tool? I actually like both, but the great thing about a clicker is that your dog never hears that sound outside of training.

One thing I usually see is that when people use words, they aren't as consistent as the clicker sound is. For example, if you want to mark the exact moment when your dog's butt touches the floor, but the first time that happens you say "Yees" and the second time just "Yes," that in itself can be a little bit confusing for your pet. On the other hand, if you use a clicker, you are always consistent and its sound will always be the same. You can't click harder than the last time.

We also have to keep in mind that we are around our dogs almost all day long, and if we choose to use a verbal marker, we might (and most likely will, even if we are not aware of it) use that word in a normal conversation. This can sometimes mislead our dog, along with making that word lose its power. With the clicker, though, the situation is completely different, because first of all, we don't usually use this tool the same way we use words, which I believe is a huge benefit.

With that being said, we have to remember that this tool is only used when we try to teach new tricks as fast and as enjoyably as possible. After the trick is learned, we will eventually wean off both the treats and the clicker, and just say "Good boy," "Good girl," "Yes," "Good," etc. This is exactly one of the reasons why some trainers like to stick with words.

Another reason why some people, especially new dog owners or new trainers, may not find it appealing to train their dogs using a clicker is because they don't like having another tool with them while they try to teach their pets new behaviors. They don't like the idea of bringing the clicker with them. A pouch, a leash, and treats are already too much to handle from their point of view, and why bring a clicker when you have your voice with you all the time?

While there is a little bit of truth in this, and the clicker can be one extra thing to hold, I don't really see this as such a hard thing to do. After all, I don't need to hold treats in my hand if I have a pouch. The way I look at this is, "Can this tool really help me make the whole process a lot more fun and effective?" If this tool will help me train my dog faster and more efficiently, I don't mind carrying it.

I believe it is totally up to you how you want to go about it. I personally love using the clicker at first, and after a behavior is 100% reliable in different environments, I just start to use my voice. I feel that a clicker allows for more precise timing, does not include a variety of tones or repetitions, is consistent, and on top of that, it's cheap.

HOW DOES CLICKER TRAINING WORK?

Firstly, as I previously said, we have to pair the clicker sound with a reward. If we don't do this, and we click without giving a treat, a clicker remains just a simple tool that produces a sound like all those other sounds, and will mean nothing to our dog. With that being said, when first introducing this tool to our furry friend, we want to "load the clicker" or give meaning to it. Your goal at this stage should be to make your pet understand, "Hey, that clicker sound always means I will get my goodie. I want more of it."

Charging or loading the clicker happens when you click and treat a few times. Usually, 15–20 repetitions is the sweet spot. This step is simple — just click, reach for a treat, and give it to your dog. Some trainers like to throw the treat onto the ground and wait for the dog to take it. I prefer to feed the treat directly to the dog. You can try this in different environments so your dog knows that no matter where you are, when he hears the click, he will be rewarded.

Note: It is important to click first and only after that reach for a treat. We want our dog to be able to predict that whenever they hear the clicking sound, a treat is coming. We don't want our dog to focus on our body language at this point.

After a while, you will notice that whenever you click, your dog will look at you, anticipating the treat. This means that your furry friend has made the connection and now knows that a click equals a goodie. Mission accomplished.

GREAT! WE PAIRED THE CLICKER SOUND WITH A REWARD. NOW WHAT?

Now, you are ready to start teaching new tricks and behaviors, give those behaviors a cue, and let your dog know that he can earn clicks and treats.

You can lure your dog into a position, and once your dog is in that position, click, give a treat, and make this behavior very strong. You can also use the clicker to capture different behaviors that you like.

For example, if you really like it when your dog is calm and lying on the floor, click whenever your dog is calm and lying on the floor. You will often see your furry friend try to figure out what caused that click, and begin to offer behaviors in order to make that noise happen again. This is really amazing, especially when you get to the point where you want to teach your dog to eliminate outdoors.

IMPORTANT THINGS TO KNOW AND REMEMBER:

1. A clicker is neither a reward nor a command either. A clicker is just a marker that **will help you capture that exact moment** when your dog did what you wanted him to do (e.g. If you want your pet to sit, the moment your dog's butt touches the floor is the exact moment that will get a click).
2. The clicker sound is distinct and **takes on meaning only after you pair that noise with a treat or something that your dog really like.** Don't use the clicker unless you give treats/something that your dog really loves. This rule must never be broken, even if gave your dog a click that you didn't mean. Which leads me to number 3.
3. You can use other words. You can just say words like "Yes, Good, Good boy, Good Girl." I personally don't like using other markers just because a clicker is distinct, easy to use, and on top, cheap. Unlike the word "Yes," which you might use it in your day to day life**, a clicker is only used in your training sessions or when you want to capture good behaviors** (e.g. when your dog is laying on the floor and being calm).
4. **Click first and only after that reach for a treat**. When charging the clicker, our purpose is to get our dog to understand that a click=something good, something positive. You don't want your pet to focus on body language at this point.
5. After you paired the clicker with a reward it's time to have fun and use this tool to teach your dog new things. **There are two ways you can go about it:**

10

a) With the help of food, lure your dog into the right positions, click and give a treat (we will have an entire section about how you can do that).
b) Capture good behaviors that are worthwhile and deserves a click (i.e. when you have guests, but your dog is really calm and polite).

PROBLEM #1 WHERE TO FIND CLICKERS AND A TREAT POUCH

YOU ARE FREE TO CHOOSE WHATEVER YOU WANT AND LIKE

First of all, I need to start off by saying I am not sponsored by any of these companies, and you are free to go with whatever you think is best for you.

TWO TOOLS THAT CAN MAKE YOUR LIFE A LOT EASIER

There are two tools that will make your life much easier when you decide to start clicker training your pet:

1. A clicker.

2. A dog training pouch/waist bag.

I have to mention that these two tools are not a must. You can train your dog without them — for example, you can use a clicker app and, instead of a pouch, just stick your treats in your pocket. But if you want to take it to the next level, you should buy a decent clicker (which is inexpensive) and a dog training pouch. These two will be the perfect tools to help your dog learn new behaviors faster, and also make your life easier.

A CLICKER CAN BE THE WAY TO GO BUT IS NOT THE ONLY WAY

Using a clicker app can be a good option, but you will often notice that you need to pay a little bit of attention to the phone as well. This can distract you from focusing on the right timing, and on your dog in general. You will also notice that an app sometimes is not as loud as it should be, which may be a problem when you take your dog outside. It really depends on you and how serious you are about this. My belief is that at first you can start using a clicker app, and once you buy the clicker, you can switch to the real tool.

WHAT CLICKER SHOULD YOU BUY

From my point of view, any clicker will get the job done (unless it is too loud and will cause your dog to be scared of that click noise. If this is the case, you can put that clicker in your pocket or just muffle it). With that being said, the best option would be to see the clicker before you buy it. You can go to your local pet shop and test a few of the clickers available. See what you think would be ideal for your dog.

The second option is to purchase one from Amazon. So, let's talk a little bit about what models are available and what I think could be the perfect fit for you.

A few years ago, the only clicker we had access to was the box clicker. This was the only design available. Besides the fact that you had to muffle it when you first wanted to charge the clicker and get your dog used to it (if you had a dog that got scared easily), use it in your pocket, and deal with it not being too comfortable in your hand because of its shape (it has a boxy design and can dig into the flesh of your palm when used for too long), this model was a great one.

Here is the link where you can check this model out. If clicking on "Here" doesn't work,   just copy and paste this onto your search bar https://www.amazon.com/dp/B0006344B2/?tag=2185-20

Note: I highly recommend this model if your dog is not able to hear well, but I don't recommend it for noise-sensitive dogs who get scared easily. I also don't recommend this model if you plan to have long training sessions or if you are a woman who has sensitive hands.

Another model you can try, especially if your dog gets scared easily, is this one (paste and search this link into your browser if clicking on "this one" doesn't work):
https://www.amazon.com/dp/B07K2BYY98/?tag=2185-20

Contrary to the box model, this one has an elastic strap located on the back so you can stretch it over your finger, which makes it very handy.

You can also try this one:
https://www.amazon.com/dp/B071NTVXN2/?tag=2185-20. This model comes with a wristband and is very comfortable.

To wrap it up, I believe that no one can tell you with 100% certainty which clicker will suit your dog best. You just have to test and see for yourself. But, as I said earlier, almost any clicker will get the job done.

TREAT POUCH

Great. Now that we talked about clickers, let's see why having a dog training pouch will help you tremendously.

Your main purpose should be to reward a good behavior as quickly as possible. A treat pouch will help you do exactly that. For me, a great pouch needs, first and foremost, to be easy to get treats out of. There are a lot of choices and products on the market. That's why we need to see again what we are about and what we are looking for.

HOW A GOOD POUCH/ WAIST BAG SHOULD LOOK LIKE

From my point of view, a good treat pouch should look similar to this one: https://amzn.to/3d2Zkn0
Or this one: https://amzn.to/2Aof2fq

You don't need anything fancier than these two. What we are looking for when buying a pouch is something practical, durable, and easy to use. As in the clicker case, I don't think you can really go wrong with these choices. I also need to mention that it is up to you what you choose.

Note: You can still have a fun time working with your dog even if you don't own these tools, but if you want to maximize efficiency and enjoy your training sessions more, buying these two can certainly help you.

IMPORTANT THINGS TO KNOW AND REMEMBER:

You don't need a clicker to start clicker training. You can use a clicker app, and after you decide to upgrade, just switch to the real one. Also, a training pouch is not a must, you can put your treats in your pocket, but if you want to make your experience a lot better, I highly recommend investing in these two items.

There are two options when you want to purchase a clicker or a training pouch. The first and most ideal is to go to your local pet shop and see these tools before you purchase them. The second is to order them from Amazon.

PROBLEM #2 WHAT TYPE OF TREATS SHOULD YOU USE

THE BASICS

When people first start training their pets using the clicker, they usually do not pay much attention to treats and their importance. I believe that treats can make a huge difference between a mediocre/good training session and a successful one.

Working with your dog, even if you do not have the right kind of treats, is still better than doing nothing. But if you really want to take your training to the next level, you have to make sure you are using the right type of treats and that your dog can't wait to work for you. If your dog doesn't like the treat you are using, it is really hard to make him pay attention.

Being aware of how your dog behaves when you first start training him is very important if you really want to change things around and eventually teach him difficult tricks. If you notice your dog doesn't pay attention to you, and he does not enjoy working with you, you need to change your approach. **Remember that our treats are the way we "pay"/reward our dog.**

PRETTY MUCH LIKE HUMANS

Dogs are pretty much like humans. Why would we work at something if there is no reward in it? We don't go to the gym for mediocre or good results. We go to the gym and put that much work in because we know that one day, we will look the way we want to look (i.e., get our reward).

The same thing happens with your dog. Why would your pet put so much work in if there are only mediocre rewards for him? Making sure your dog considers your reward valuable/worth working for is crucial.

When talking about "treats," we don't talk just about food. A reward can be anything that your pet likes, such as getting a deep scratch behind the ears, playing, taking him to the park, or just a simple praise.

THE REASON WHY I THINK THERE IS NO SUCH THING AS FADING OUT REWARDS COMPLETELY

This is exactly the reason why I do not believe in fully weaning off treats. Yes, you can, for sure, get to the level where your dog is performing well without giving him food treats, but you still need to give your pet something. It can be a "good boy" or "good girl," but no matter what, you need to keep reinforcing the behaviors you like.

Although a reward can mean a walk or playing, when you try to teach your dog something new using the clicker, the most convenient way to go about it is not to give a toy or play with him. I have found that this will sometimes take more time and distract your dog from what you are trying to teach in the first place.

A FEW IMPORTANT THINGS WE NEED TO CONSIDER

A few more things we can discuss when we're talking about food treats are:

Treats need to be adjusted depending on what tricks you're trying to teach (i.e., just a simple sit or something more difficult) and the environment you are working in (i.e., at home or in crowded places).

Food treats mean more calories. This is exactly why we need to either change our dog's meal portion to balance out what we are using for treats, or simply use his food (i.e., kibble).

Treat size must be small. As in the case with playing or giving our dog a toy, we don't want our dog to lose focus and start chewing on our treats. You can still have delicious treats even if you keep them very small.

TAKE THE GUESS OUT OF EQUATION. LET YOUR DOG SHOW YOU

I believe the best approach when you try to figure out what types of treats you should use is to stop guessing what you think would work best and just let your dog tell you what he likes the most. Every dog is different, and while some dogs will accept and work just with their daily kibble, others may not.

Your purpose regarding those very short training sessions is to get your dog's attention and keep it. This is exactly why I think having multiple treats with you will be an advantage. Think about it — if your pet loses interest in working with you and you have five different types of treats, you can try switching them and see if you can make your pet pay attention again.

WHAT TYPES OF TREAT USUALLY WORK BEST?

Usually, treats that are home cut-up/perishable work best, especially when you are trying to teach your pet new tricks or when you are working with him in a crowded place. For example, if you have used kibble to teach your dog to "sit" and you were at home, you may want to switch to cheese when your dog is in the park or around other dogs (i.e., high-distraction places).

But, let's keep it real, using perishable treats is not always practical, especially if you are very busy or you don't want to cook. Although these kinds of treats work best, cheese, liverwurst, deli meats, diced chicken, diced hot dogs, steak, etc. — because a lot of people nowadays are very busy, using your dog's daily food (kibble or perishable) can be a good option.

The benefit is these treats are already cut up and you can take them everywhere you go without worrying about them going bad. You just take them out of the bag, stick them into your training pouch and you're good to go. Don't forget, whatever you want to use, keeping your dog engaged should be your purpose, and the best way to do this is by switching things around once in a while.

19

IMPORTANT THINGS TO KNOW AND REMEMBER

1. Pay attention to your treats. **Treats can make the difference between getting results or not.** If you notice your dog is not engaged with you, something is wrong and you need to change things up.

2. Being aware of how your dog reacts when you are trying to teach new behaviors is key. **Pay attention and he will tell you.** Remember the gym example — you don't go to the gym to look mediocre, you go to the gym because you know the results are worthwhile. That's why you put the work in upfront.

3. **Don't wean off "treats" completely.** Yes, at some point you might be able to wean off food completely, but you need to replace it with something your dog really loves. It can be praise, a play session, or anything else, but never stop reinforcing behaviors you have built and worked so hard on.

4. **If you ask your dog to do something more difficult, pay him more.** Don't forget the example with training your dog at home and training in a crowded place — increase the value of treats as you raise the criteria.

5. **Let your dog show you exactly what he likes and enjoys.** Your dog will show you precisely what will work for him — just pay attention.

PROBLEM #3 GETTING DEEPER IN USING OTHER MARKERS AND WORDS

BACK TO THE BASICS

We have already covered this subject, but because a lot of people seem to get a little confused about it, I wanted to dedicate an entire chapter to this matter and try to go even deeper. If we fully understand what "clicker training" is (by now we should have), how it works, and why we use a clicker in the first place, then answering this question is just a matter of simplicity.

A lot of people are very skeptical when they first hear about clicker training. Why should I use a clicker? Why can't I just use my mouth? Can I use a pen instead of a clicker? Wouldn't snapping my fingers do the same thing? Could I use a clicker app and still get the same effect? Why not simply say "Good dog/Good girl?" or "Yes?" Couldn't I just use my tongue? These are just a few of the questions folks usually have.

First and foremost, as I already said right from the start, **a clicker is nothing else but an event marker.** A click is a signal that lets the dog understand exactly what behavior has caused him to receive a treat.

Simply put, a clicker is just a small mechanical noisemaker that we use to tell our dogs precisely which behavior we liked, and to give a reward. It is like you're saying, "Hey, I really loved what you did right there, and that's why I'm going to reward you," or "A goodie is coming."

A clicker is just a clicker, it is not magical. The meaning we give to that clicker is where the magic happens. **This is exactly why giving a treat every time you click is a must.**

CAN WE REALLY USE SOMETHING ELSE INSTEAD OF THE CLICKER?

Now, back to our subject, can we use something else instead of a clicker? The simple answer to this question is YES, of course you can use something else.

If you want, for example, the word "YES" to be your marker, you will have to pair the word "yes" with the meaning "I really liked that one and a treat is coming for you."

WHY SOME TRAINERS DON'T LIKE USING A CLICKER

There are many trainers who don't like using a clicker because, first of all, you have to own a clicker (which is inexpensive) and then you have to carry that clicker with you wherever you go (or so they think).

They usually say that you have your voice with you all the time, but you don't have clickers with you all the time, so why use one? They sometimes forget that, as I already mentioned, we only use clickers to teach new tricks or behaviors. After your pet is reliably performing 100%, we wean off the clicker and just praise the dog. "Well then why have one, if in the end it is still your voice that you end up using?" Because our purpose is not only to teach new things in an easy and fun way, but to make this whole process as fast as possible.

A FEW OTHER TOOLS YOU CAN USE TO REPLACE THE CLICKER

Yes, of course you can use your tongue, as long as you keep it consistent. But don't you think that you might get a bit tired after one training session? Yes, of course you can use your fingers, but you might need to use your fingers 50–100 times per session, and it can be a little hard to be consistent.

As I already said, the benefit of using a clicker instead of saying "Yes," for example, may simply be that a clicker will always sound the same, but if you say "Yeees" and you're excited, and the next time you just say "Yes," it might be a little confusing for the dog. He might now think that he did a better job the first time, and can get a little disappointed. On the other hand, with a clicker you are always consistent. You can't click louder than the last time.

With that being said, I do believe you can use a clicker app, a pen, blow a whistle, or cluck your tongue, but in many cases, a clicker is the most convenient and inexpensive way.

IMPORTANT THINGS TO KNOW AND REMEMBER:

1. A clicker **is nothing else but an event marker**, it is not magical. If you believe you can stay consistent with the word "Yes," use this word as your marker. If you believe you can be consistent with something else, use that tool.
2. A few new trainers and dog owners don't like having a clicker because they have to carry that clicker with them, and why do so if, in the end, it is still your voice that you will end up using? Also, in many of these cases, people are either holding treats in their hand or they don't have a waist bag. Once you buy a pouch and get rid of the food, **you are free to carry whatever you want that has the potential to help you get better with your training**, it is not a big deal.

PROBLEM #4 CAN YOU CLICK WITHOUT GIVING A TREAT?

MOST COMMON QUESTIONS PEOPLE HAVE

Another subject we have to cover is clicking without giving a treat. The most common questions people have when clicking and giving treats are:

1. Let's say my dog does something well (e.g., lying down and being good), and I click — should I give a treat as well?
2. If I don't have treats in the moment, but my dog does something well, should I still use the clicker?
3. After my dog is used to the clicker, can I click without giving a treat?
4. Will my pet think it's getting a treat every time? Will it be the only way my dog will learn? If, for example, my dog does something I like and I don't click, will he be confused? Will my dog think he will get a treat every time he does something I ask, or will he only listen to me if I click and have a treat??

BACK TO THE BASICS

The most important thing **we need to remember** is that the clicker is just a training tool we use to communicate with our dog. The clicker itself doesn't have much meaning to our dog, it's just a sound. The clicker **only becomes meaningful after we associate that sound with a goodie, treat, or something our dog enjoys**. Only after a clicker becomes a conditioned reinforcer can we use it for teaching our dogs different cues.

A FEW THINGS WE SHOULD NEVER DO

First and foremost, we should never click without giving a treat. **Every time you click, it is crucial that you deliver a treat, even if you didn't plan that click.** When your pet performs the behavior you want, but you don't deliver a treat, you first confuse the dog and, secondly, the clicker will lose its meaning.

The right way to wean off of treats is not by clicking and not rewarding. As we will talk about in the "wean off of treats" chapter, the approach you want to use is to gradually skip clicking/giving a food treat, and just give a praise" e.g. Good boy/ Good girl."

Your pet should think that he will get a treat every time you click, that's the power of the clicker, so don't try to wean off treats by using the tool but not giving a reward.

IMPORTANT THINGS TO KNOW AND REMEMBER:

We need to always remember that a click = a reward. Weaning off the clicker/treats must be done correctly (this subject will be covered in the "Wean Off Treats" chapter). If you try to get rid of treats by clicking but not rewarding, the clicker will lose its meaning.

PROBLEM #5 THE PERFECT AGE TO START CLICKER TRAINING

THERE IS A PERFECT TIME?

We already know how clicker training works. We are all set, we have a clicker, a pouch, and we know everything we need to know about treats. Now, the question is: When should you start training your puppy? How old should the puppy be? What is the perfect age?

The answer is: **There is no perfect age**. You need to start working with your puppy as soon as possible. The sooner you start, the better.

Think about this, why should your puppy spend his energy on destructive things when you can give your pup a constructive way to use it? It doesn't matter if your pup is 8 weeks old or 11 weeks old, start as soon as possible

.

TRAINING A PUPPY SHOULD BE FUN

You will quickly realize that training your pup is fun, and you can have them performing new tricks in no time. It is fascinating to see how a pup evolves when using a clicker to train them. You will also see that they will try to figure out why and what causes that click, and they will be trying to do tricks on their own just to receive a treat and capture your attention.

Note: Training sessions with your puppy should be fun and enjoyable for both of you. I strongly believe that training your dog with a clicker will help you a lot, and with its help, you can have a great dog that is well-behaved and has great habits.

IMPORTANT THINGS TO KNOW AND REMEMBER:

1. There is no perfect age, start training your puppy using a clicker as soon as you bring him home.
2. Make it fun, you will soon notice that your pet can't wait to get another click.

PROBLEM #6 HOW LONG ONE TRAINING SESSION CAN BE AND HOW MANY SESSIONS PER DAY

First of all, we have to keep in mind that consistency is the key. You can't really go to the gym for 10 hours one day, and then completely skip training and eating right for the next 6 days. You need to be consistent and do it every day. If we are consistent and go to the gym for 1 hour every day, in time, those hours will add up, and our body, whether we realize it or not, will start to change

LONG SESSIONS VS SHORT SESSIONS

The same situation applies with our dogs. I truly believe that several short sessions are much better than one long session. The best approach is to keep the duration of a training session very short. If your training sessions are short and effective, the results can improve drastically, but if you try to make them as long as possible, chances are your dog will lose interest and get bored.

HOW MANY SESSIONS PER DAY?

As far as sessions per day, try to see what works for you and for your dog, it can really depend on how much time you have available. Usually, 4–10 sessions can work really well if your sessions are not too long.

IMPORTANT THINGS TO KNOW AND REMEMBER:

1. Keep those training sessions **very short and effective**, consistency is the key.
2. Try to have 4–10 short sessions per day. Don't forget, **short sessions are better** than long, boring sessions.

PROBLEM #7 YOU SAW THIS BOOK AND YOU BOUGHT IT, BUT YOUR PET IS NOT A PUPPY ANYMORE

IS IT REALLY YOUR DOG TOO OLD TO START CLICKER TRAINING?

Maybe you saw a YouTube video about clicker training, you read an article, or your friend told you about this method. The problem is, your dog is not a puppy anymore. You either didn't know about clicker training when you brought him home, you rescued him from the pound, or you simply didn't have time for training when your dog was a pup. The question is, is it possible to train your adult dog?

Yes, it is not too late. You can start training your dog any time, at any age. Don't let yourself be fooled by the idea that your dog is somehow too old to start clicker training. It is never too late. You need to start just as you would if you had a puppy

JUST STICK TO THE BASICS

You just need to teach him what the click means, or as we often say, "load the clicker." After that, you are good to go. It is exactly as in the puppy case — once you click and your dog starts looking for the treat, it means he got the idea that a click = a goodie. In conclusion, I'm sure that even if your dog is 5, 7, or 8 years old, he would love this tool and those clicker training sessions.

IMPORTANT THINGS TO KNOW AND REMEMBER:

1. It is never too late to start training your dog with a clicker. Stick to the basics, "charge" the clicker first, and start training your dog as if you had a puppy.

PROBLEM #8 WHEN AND HOW TO ADD A CUE TO A BEHAVIOR

WHEN TO ADD A CUE (WORD/VISUAL SIGN) TO A SPECIFIC BEHAVIOR

First and foremost, the cue must be added after your dog can 100% perform the behavior you want to name or add a visual sign to. Therefore, after you see your dog can do the behavior without hesitation, it's time to pair a word or visual sign to that move.

WHAT YOU'RE GOING TO PAIR THAT BEHAVIOR WITH? A VISUAL SIGN OR A WORD?

Most people will go with pairing a word to a specific behavior, while some, especially those that have a dog with hearing problems, will have to use a visual sign. It is totally up to you how you want to go about it, but you need to choose something that you will always use from now on when you want your dog to perform that specific movement.

WAIT FOR YOUR DOG TO DO THAT BEHAVIOR AND USE YOUR CUE

Let's say the behavior you want to teach will be something really basic, like a "SIT."

1. Start by warming up your dog. Wait for your dog to sit and as soon as your dog's butt touches the floor, give him a click and a treat.

2. Repeat this 10–15 times, let your pet know what you want from him.

31

3. After your dog is warmed up, start to pair that movement with a word or visual sign just as, or while, your dog starts doing it.

4. Environment will play a huge role in how your furry friend will be able to perform, that's why I believe the best way to start is to train your dog in a place where there are no distractions (e.g., your home), and then, after your dog is 100% reliable, change the environment and try to make it more difficult (i.e., train your dog in the park or a crowded place).

Note: Remember, (a) warm up your dog a few times, (b) as your dog starts to perform that trick, just use the word you chose or your visual sign. It should look like this: (1) Dog starts to perform, (2) you use your cue, (3) dog's butt touches the floor, (4) you give a click and a treat.

The more you practice, the better. You need to understand that every dog is different, some dogs will get it faster than others. Patience is the key.

SOME DOG TRAINERS CHOOSE TO ADD A VISUAL/ HAND SIGN CUE FIRST

Dogs tend to be more visually oriented than verbally oriented. This is the reason why some trainers like to teach their dogs what they want from them by just using a hand signal at first, and after the pet gets it, they begin introducing the word too. The goal with this approach should be to make it easier for your dog at first, because you are using a hand signal, but in the end to just say the cue, so you don't have to lift up your right arm for your dog to understand he must sit while you are in the park, that's ridiculous.

If you decide to do the visual sign before your chosen word, you must follow the exact same steps taught in the "Wait for Your Dog to Do the Behavior and Use Your Cue" section, but instead of adding a word while your dog starts to sit, you just use your hand signal. As far as the environment, the rules are the same. You must choose a place with no distractions at all at first, and after your dog is 100% reliable in that quiet place, switch to a crowded one. To make sure your dog really knows what that cue means, try it cold once in a while. If your dog is able to perform the moment you ask out of the blue, it means he got it.

HOW TO ADD THE SECOND CUE/ YOUR CHOSEN WORD FOR THAT SPECIFIC BEHAVIOR

After you realize your dog is reliable 100% using your hand signal, it is time to add your second cue. The right way to do this is to just insert the word cue before your visual cue. This should look like this:

(1) Say "Sit," (2) make the visual sign, (3) dog's butt touches the floor, (4) you give a click and a treat.

FADE OUT THE VISUAL SIGN

After a while, stop using your hand signal, and just say "Sit." Practice this a few times and see how your dog performs.

Tip: If you really want to make sure you keep both cues strong, switch them around. One time ask your dog to sit by just raising your hand, and the next time just say the word.

HOW ABOUT TEACHING MORE DIFFICULT TRICKS

Great, we now know how to add a cue when you are trying to teach your dog something really basic, like a sit, but what do you do when you want to teach your dog other, more difficult tricks?

Some trainers like to use food to "lure" the pet into the right position. Although this is a great strategy, you must be careful when you're using it. The problem with this technique is that if you don't use it wisely, your dog will perform that behavior only when he sees food in your hand. This is exactly the reason why a lot of people get frustrated and state things like "My dog is only treat motivated," "My dog only listens when there are treats in my hand," or "My puppy only focuses on the treat and never gives me eye contact."

They are right, their pets only listen when there is food because they did not pay attention to what they were doing in the first place, and somehow they contributed to creating this habit.

33

If you have already fallen into this trap, you will see that when asking your dog to sit, for example, but you don't have any treats in your hand, your furry friend will look at you like you're crazy. He just won't perform. I found that the main reason why this is happening is because you "lured" your dog into the right position with the use of food, and your dog now got used to it. It is a habit — he sees your hand with treats and he performs. You didn't level up your game, and your dog is a brilliant one, he knows it.

THE RIGHT APPROACH

The right approach is to switch things around. Yes, use treats to lure your pet into the right positions, but after 2 or 3 times of trial, level up. Just pretend you have food, even if you don't, and use the same hand signal to get your dog into the right position. What I mean by this is, do what you usually do for only 2 or 3 times, let your dog follow the treat until he is in the right position. Click, and give a treat once that happens.

The fourth time, just pretend you have a treat in your hand and do the exact same gesture as you did the first time, but when your dog is in the right position, just show him that there is no treat in your hand. Click, take a treat out of your pouch, and give it to your pet.

Note: The most important thing in this equation is to just show your pet that there is no treat in your hand.

LEVEL IT UP EVEN FURTHER

To level things up even further, show your dog right from the start that you don't have any treat in your hand. After that, use your hand the same way as you did before and get your furry friend into the right position. Once your dog is in the right position, click and give a treat.

You can, and need to, be creative with this, try to always make it harder and harder for your pet. Don't get comfortable using just one technique. Make your visual signals less obvious and increase the difficulty.

Keep in mind that patience is key, if your dog stops doing the behavior you're trying to teach, just go back and make a clearer visual sign.

IMPORTANT THINGS TO KNOW AND REMEMBER:

1. Add your cue <u>only after</u> your dog can 100% perform that behavior.
2. Decide <u>what your cue will be</u>, a visual sign, a word or both?
3. Pair the cue just as or <u>while your dog starts doing that behavior</u>.
4. When you're trying to teach your pet more difficult tricks, lure your dog into the right position. After that, try to level things up as described in this chapter.

PROBLEM #9 HOW TO CLICKER TRAIN TWO DOGS

IS CLICKER TRAINING CHALLENGING WHEN YOU HAVE TWO DOGS?

Even if clicker training can be very effective and useful for teaching your dog new behaviors, it can also be a little bit challenging when you have multiple dogs. How can we be sure your older dog isn't getting signals crossed when you are training your puppy? Should you separate them while introducing the clicker, or can you train them together? If you train one and the other hears the click, but is not receiving any treats, wouldn't that desensitize him to the clicker?

THE BEST THING YOU CAN DO

First of all, the best thing you can do for your puppy, to really help him understand as fast and easily as possible precisely what you want and the behavior that you expect, is to train your pet in an environment where there are very few distractions or no distractions at all. You want your dog's attention to be on you, and what you are trying to teach. If there is another dog, a child, or it's really noisy, it is very hard for your furry friend to keep his focus.

With that being said, I believe that, while introducing the clicker, you need to separate them. Eventually, you will be able to train them together and they will understand who's clicking who, but I feel like in the beginning it can be a little confusing. So the first thing is to just completely separate them. "Completely" meaning to the point where the dog you are not working with won't hear the clicker noise.

For example, let one dog outside (in the yard) while the one you are working with is indoors. This way, you can know for sure that only one is playing and is totally isolated, while the other is performing and learning new tricks.

Dogs are very smart, and they can quickly figure out how things work. You will soon realize, especially when a dog is well trained and really understands you, that he can pretty much learn what you like and what you will reward. After a while, when you put your pets together, you will start to notice they can understand really fast who is getting clicked and who is not. This is exactly the reason I think that after you train each dog separately, they will get used to you, what you like, what you don't, how you talk, and when you're addressing them.

Therefore, when you decide to start training them together, you will see that your dogs will learn to discern really fast whom you are looking at and figure out what behavior got a treat. For example, if "Jack" and "Duke" were already trained by you, they both know it is much more likely for you to click if they sit or behave well. If "Jack" is doing something well, but "Duke" is doing something wrong and you click, yes, at first they might both look for the treat, but when "Duke" sees that only "Jack" received one, he will start to figure out that whatever he was doing was incorrect.

HOW TO MAKE THIS A LOT EASIER FOR YOUR DOG

Many people want to make this much easier for the dog, and you can for sure do that, but you must be willing to put a little bit more effort in.

Your first option will be to buy a clicker that has different tones or sounds. This will take a little bit more effort from your part, because you have to always make sure you use the same unique sound for rewarding and giving a treat to "Dog A" and not mix it up with "Dog B's" sound.

Note: If you don't pay attention to what you are doing, you can hit the wrong button, which can turn out to be really confusing.

The second option is to use a different verbal marker for "Dog A" and something else for "Dog B" (e.g., you can choose to praise "Dog A" with a "click + good boy" and "Dog B" with "click way to go").

As in the first case, the main thing is to always remember that "good boy" is for "Dog A" and "way to go" is for "Dog B." **Switching these words can cause confusion, which is not great.**

WHAT I WILL CHOOSE IF I HAD TO

Personally, this is the option I would choose if I had to pick between buying a clicker with different tones or just using different verbal markers. The reason behind it is that our goal is, at some point, to wean off the clicker and food treats anyway, that's why I feel like this will help us a lot in moving forward with our plan.

DON'T OVERTHINK IT DOGS ARE BRILLIANT

You should always remember that dogs are really smart. They will get used to you and the behaviors that you like, and this is the reason why I like to let them figure out for themselves who got a click and who did not. At first, this may be too difficult to do, but after a few sessions your dogs will catch up.

However, if you decide that you want to make it as simple as possible for the dog, just go with a clicker that has different sounds. You can buy this kind of clicker at PetSmart.

BE CREATIVE

When using these techniques, be creative. If you already own two box clickers, for example, you can just drill a hole in one of your clicker's metal parts. This will make the clicker you drill sound different.

DON'T FORGET WHAT WE HAVE LEARNED IN THE CHAPTER REGARDING TREATS

Once you find that your dogs are individually reliable, and you decide to start working with them at the same time, in the same place, you want to make things interesting and not forget that the purpose is to have fun. You need to enjoy training sessions, and dogs need to enjoy them too. That's why you always have to keep in mind what we learned regarding treats. You want to reward your dog based on the difficulty of the cue you ask your dog to perform.

If, for example, "Dog A" is the dog you are working with, and "Dog B" is the one waiting, you should always pay the second dog a much higher treat (e.g., maybe you ask "Dog A" to sit or do some other tricks, while you want "Dog B" to be calm and wait on a mat until you finish the session with your first pet. You give your working pet daily food as a treat, while the second one, the one that is waiting, should have some chicken). This is just an example of how you can go about it and make sure your sessions are not interrupted just because one of your dogs is jealous.

YOU CAN STILL CLICKER TRAIN EVEN IF YOU HAVE TWO DOGS

Keep in mind, you can still clicker train even if you have two dogs. You only need to have more patience and try to gradually improve things. Don't expect your dogs to get it in the first second, but also don't underestimate how brilliant these animals are. Your dogs can for sure figure out what you expect from them, and you can, without a doubt, train them both.

Tip: Teach your dogs how to be polite and how to wait, and your training sessions will improve a lot.

IMPORTANT THINGS TO KNOW AND REMEMBER:

1. When you first start to clicker train your puppy, the best thing to do is to completely separate him from the other dog. Choose a quiet place.
2. If you want to make it easier for your dogs, you can either buy a clicker with different tones/ sounds or just use a different verbal marker.
3. Don't overthink it, dogs are brilliant. Once they get used with you, they can quickly figure out who's clicking who.
4. Reward your dog based on the difficulty of the cue (i.e. if' Dog B" is the one waiting the whole time, pay him a higher value).

PROBLEM #10 HOW TO POTTY TRAIN A DOG USING A CLICKER

AT THIS POINT THEY DON'T KNOW ANY BETTER

One of the most important and difficult parts of owning a dog is teaching him where to eliminate. Although this is a book about clicker training, I chose to write about this matter because I feel like a lot of people who get into clicker training often wonder how you can potty train using the clicker.

The problem with your pups is that sometimes they don't realize that the spot they chose for peeing or pooping is not the ideal one, at least not for you. They do not care yet about where they should eliminate, so wherever they are, if they need to go, they will go.

The good news is we can use our clicker the same way we used it to teach our dog a new trick. As long as the clicker is a communication tool that tells your dog "Yes, I really like what you did," we won't have that many problems when we try to tell and show our dog where we want him to eliminate.

WHEN TO CLICK? WHY TIMING IS IMPORTANT?

What gets rewarded gets repeated, and this is huge when we talk about potty training.

The best thing you can do is to prepare. This means when you decide to take your puppy to the place you want him to eliminate, you need to take your pouch and the clicker with you.

41

Secondly, you need to really understand the power of timing. **Clicking before or during your pup's elimination is a huge mistake**.

If you are careful and pay attention to the moment when your pet is done, your chances of instilling this habit go through the roof. If not, chances are your dog will get really excited because of the click and will stop. This could end with them doing it in the wrong place.

The bottom line: if you want to quickly teach your pet where to eliminate, click and give praise plus a goodie once you are sure your pup is done.

OTHER TIPS THAT WILL HELP YOU AND YOUR DOG

A few more tips that will also help you with your potty training are to first of all sit down, take your time, and:

1. Create a feeding schedule. A dog usually needs to go out after every single meal.

2. After creating your dog's feeding schedule, create a "go out/potty break" schedule.

Working on your dog's feeding and potty break schedule should make your life a whole lot easier. The ideal situation will be for you to teach your puppy (at a very early age) where you want him to go.

However, there are dogs that didn't get the chance to learn this at a very early age, which is why you have to work with what you have. Change patterns, create a feeding and potty break schedule. This should help. It doesn't matter if your dog is a puppy or not, you can still teach new behaviors using the clicker as well as giving him praise and treats.

Keep in mind:

1. When going outside, try to always take the dog to the same spot he went last time.

2. Make your dog understand that potty breaks are potty breaks, not walks. You want to reward your dog for going potty outside, not punish him. If you take your dog for a walk but suddenly decide to end it as soon as your dog has eliminated, your pet may force himself not to go potty during walks anymore. He may start

42

to think that this will cause you to go back home, which can be the reason why he will eliminate at home and try to hold it as much as he can.

3. Don't forget about telling your dog what a good job he did. Make it huge. This goes hand in hand with not scolding your puppy for accidents, at least in the beginning.

COMMON MISTAKES

1. Punishing your dog. Don't punish your puppy or adult dog for mistakes. Your pet needs to fully understand what you want from him. Punishing your pet will only make things worse. Be consistent and have patience, your dog will start to trust you more and more.

2. Not using the clicker the same way you did to teach new tricks or behaviors. Use the clicker the same way as you did to teach your dog to "sit." Come up with a cue, and when your dog has finished eliminating, use that cue.

3. Not paying enough attention to your dog's health. Make sure your dog is healthy and there are no problems. This is very important. If your dog already knows where he needs to go to eliminate but is having accidents, that's a good sign something isn't right.

4. Forgetting the fact that your dog wants the same thing as you. Keep in mind that dogs prefer to live in a clean environment. At this point, they just don't know any better, that's all, but with your help, they can learn in no time.

Note: Whatever you do, don't get mad and reprimand your pet if he is having accidents. It happens. Clean up and move on. Focus on what you want and what you would like to see in the future. Punishing your dog will make things worse.

HOW TO CLEAN UP AND WHAT TO USE

When cleaning up, make sure to use products specifically for pet feces and urine. The reason behind this is because we don't want your dog to detect a smell and eliminate again in the same place. Be sure you clean up as well as you can, and don't forget that dogs have a better sense of smell than humans do.

IMPORTANT THINGS TO KNOW AND REMEMBER:

1. <u>Don't get mad and don't punish your puppy,</u> at this point they don't know any better.
2. Keep in mind that timing is super important, click after you are sure your dog has finished.
3. Create a feeding and a potty break schedule.
4. Be patient and don't forget that your dog prefers to live in a clean environment as well.

PROBLEM #11 WEANING OFF OF TREATS

WHAT WE NEED TO KNOW

When people first hear about clicker training or training with a clicker, they often don't understand how it actually works.

They sometimes get worried and start to think that if they teach their puppy a good behavior or trick using a clicker and treats, they will now have to use food or this tool all the time.

After a behavior is learned and well-established, meaning that the dog actually performs reliably when you give the cue or command, you can begin to wean off the clicker and the food. We also need to remember that even if we try to get rid of the clicker and treats, a click should still mean a treat every time.

Weaning off the clicker should be done gradually. You can't suddenly go from clicking and giving treats every single time the pet performs well, to not giving anything. You need to click and treat intermittently, then occasionally, to keep the behavior strong.

THE GOOD WAY AND THE BAD WAY

There is a good way to wean off treats, and there is a bad way. If your approach is not thoughtful, you can cause a behavior to break down completely. **Our purpose should always be to maintain that good behavior we worked so hard to teach in the first place.**

You should only start weaning off treats for behaviors that are solid. Keep in mind that how a dog performs a behavior can also be influenced by the environment. This means that, for example, if you give a cue and your dog performs it well at home, you can begin to slowly reduce treats there, but you can't expect the same results right away in a new, more distracting environment.

The environment is different, distractions are different, so you have to work your way up. With that being said, we also have to talk about not completely weaning off treats. As mentioned earlier, distractions and environment play a huge role in this process.

For example, if your dog is doing really well in the park or in crowded places, where it is much harder to focus, but still behaves beautifully, why wouldn't you reward him? It's not a bad thing to reward your pet periodically for behaviors you like. Your dog can behave well without treats, but giving him one once in a while will help maintain that behavior.

HOW IT WORKS IN REAL LIFE

Now that we have covered the basics, let's see how to go about it in real life.

Let's say that you are at home and your dog is performing a trick perfectly. You give him the cue "sit," his butt touches the floor quickly, you click or praise, and give a treat.

He knows the cue well, performs flawlessly, and you think it's time to wean off treats. The effective way to do this is to ask him to "sit" four more times, and on the fifth time skip the click and treat, and just say "good boy" or "good girl" or whatever praise you normally use.

Next time, you might ask for the behavior five times and skip the reward on the sixth. You'll be rewarding about 8 out of 10 commands. From here, watch your dog to see if this approach works and whether he still responds well. If he does, move to 7 out of 10.

GO RANDOM AND DON'T MAKE A PATTERN OUT OF THIS

The principle is the same — go randomly and avoid creating a pattern. You want your dog to guess when the treat is coming. If 7 out of 10 works, move to 6 out of 10, and continue until food treats are faded out completely.

Note: When skipping the treat, skip the click as well. A click equals a treat, and if you click without giving a treat, the clicker can lose its meaning. Also, avoid creating a predictable pattern — mix things up.

DON'T BE IN A RUSH- TAKE YOUR TIME

Don't rush to stop using the clicker and treats. The best approach is to take your time and make sure your dog doesn't give up on you. A behavior can become stronger with the right strategy, or break down if you push it too fast without paying attention to your dog.

WHAT TO DO IF YOUR DOG DOESN'T RESPOND TO CUES ANYMORE

If your dog stops responding to cues, go back to the steps you used when first teaching that behavior. You'll often find that your dog will perform again, sometimes better than before.

Many people are hesitant to start clicker training because they don't understand how to apply what we've talked about here. They fear that after teaching a behavior, they won't be able to get their dog to perform without a clicker and treats. But as mentioned earlier, once a behavior is solid, you can start weaning off treats.

NEVER STOP REWARDING YOUR DOG COMPLETELY FOR ACTIONS YOU LIKE

Even if the goal is to eliminate the clicker and food treats, there should always be some form of reward for your dog — praise, playtime, a walk, or anything you know your dog enjoys.

A dog should not work only for food, but rewarding him periodically for a job well done will make training more fun for both of you.

BONUS CHAPTERS

5 PRINCIPLES TO CORRECT BAD PUPPY BEHAVIOR WITHOUT PUNISHMENT AND THINGS TO KEEP IN MIND

Every puppy breed is different, and apart from needing to be disciplined, the type of breed that you own has a significant effect on what behavior is concerned. During the puppy stage, your pet is only getting to know you, the world, and itself, which means that they will have to learn what they can and can't do. With this in mind, when you decide to get a puppy from a breeder or if you choose to rescue one, you have to be prepared to put in a lot of effort to teach them obedience.

Puppies differ from adult dogs. They require a lot more attention with training and development habits to prevent or improve behavioral problems that, let's face it, can disrupt your life. If you can't address a puppy's behavioral issues from the start, they will become even harder to control when as an adult. This is especially the case because they have passed the stage when they are the most susceptible to learning.

Why do you want your puppy to be trained properly from a young age? Well, your puppy is like a baby. No matter the breed or size, they are still a baby and will remain in the infancy stage for at least a year or two. After the first two years, puppies slow down and become more adult-like, which means that they aren't as disruptive and all over the place anymore. Sure, they still need your attention and want to play, but much less than they used to.

If you are planning on getting a puppy or already have one, you have to consider how to treat and train them. Even though your dog is a pet and not an actual human baby, they require you to teach them the difference between right and wrong. If you don't, you will have problems with your pet for years to come.

Basic puppy training solves behavioral problems at an early stage so that you don't have to worry about it later. Many behaviors, including hyperactivity, chewing, lack of house-training, nipping, eating feces, barking excessively, or getting sick in your car, occurs because of a lack of training.

This can all be resolved by implementing the following principles to approach and treat bad behavior:

1. Be consistent.

    A lack of training and a little bit of training is equally ineffective. When you decide to address your dog's behavioral problems, you have to implement rules and strategies daily to treat bad behavior. You can't discipline your dog for chewing your shoes on Monday and skip Tuesday. The same goes for any other type of bad behavior. If you are not going to be consistent, your dog won't ever learn. By teaching them not to do something one day and treat that same thing any time after that, you are confusing your dog and nothing is retained. If your dog continues to repeat bad behavior, you may become frustrated, which will also have a negative influence on your relationship.

2. Be prompt.

    When you choose to punish your puppy is a very significant factor in your journey to training. You can't punish your pet for everything. You also can't punish them unless you catch them in the act because they will have already forgotten what they did wrong. Now, you can't always keep an eye on your puppy. So, what do you do? Well, thanks to technology, you can make use of Petcube, a camera that broadcasts your voice should you catch your dog doing something they shouldn't. Ideally, you want to spend as much time you can with your dog in the learning stage and have the people in your house train them the same way you would, but if you can't, you can always make use of alternative tools.

3. Be strict.

    When you scold your puppy or tell it 'no', you have to be straight and firm with your signals. Many people yell at their puppies out of frustration. However, dogs don't understand how to respond to stressed behavior. If they can't deal with their own stressed behavior, how are they supposed to deal with yours? When they stress or develop anxiety, they act out, which is what they will do when you show signs of aggression towards them. To become a puppy parent that knows what you are doing, you should display authority towards a puppy without losing your cool.

4. Make use of positive reinforcement.

    Just like you punish your puppy's bad behavior, you also have to reward good behavior. This is especially necessary if your dog manages to behave by itself. If your puppy stopped barking by itself, give them a treat or express how excited you are and offer pets or scratches. If your dog goes to the bathroom outside by themselves instead of inside, tell them how good they are. This goes for any behavioral problem they may become resistant towards or rectify. A little positive reinforcement goes a long way with regards to what your puppy will be doing right or wrong tomorrow.

5. Give your dog a timeout.

    Isolating your puppy seems like a terrible idea, but it's not. It's very helpful in teaching your puppy between right and wrong. Timeouts are very effective when you use them as the right response to certain behaviors. You can discipline your dog by using timeouts. This can be done by giving them signals like saying, "Oops!" when they do something wrong. Then you immediately leave the room or put them outside for no longer than a couple of minutes. It will teach them what it means to do something wrong. Your puppy will learn that there are consequences. All your puppy wants is to be close to you, so if you create a little distance due to bad behavior, they will stop doing what you don't want them to do and try to please you instead.

CAN A CLICKER SOLVE DOG-AGGRESSIVE PROBLEMS?

Something like clicker training seems like something too simple to have a significant effect on your dog. This includes treating problems they have with aggression during the puppy stage.

Ideally, aggression is something that every dog owner needs to get under control with their dog, especially when they are a puppy, because of the fact that aggressive behavior can escalate with age. Your puppy may start out tugging on shoes, biting other puppies playfully, or treating your hands as a chew-toy, but it's not a good thing to allow in the long-run. If your puppy is not trained at a young age, they could progress to biting harder or becoming more aggressive towards strangers and other dogs. With the sound, clicker training can help you solve dog-aggressive behavioral issues by informing your dog that they have done something correctly, which will result in a reward. With the help of a clicker, you can teach your dog to listen to you on-demand by making them used to listening to the clicking sound of the marker.

Like with teaching your dog to associate a treat with sitting their rear on the ground or laying down on their belly, you can also train them to associate an action with the sound of the clicker. For aggressive-behavior, you specifically want your dog to associate lying down on their belly with the reward. The reason for this is because you want to avoid your dog moving while aggressive. Instead of teaching your dog to stand still or walk towards you, you should teach them to lie down at your signal to distract them from the situation. This will help your dog listen to you more effectively by keeping its focus on you.

Food treats are used for all types of behavioral training because if you were to reward your dog with a game, like playing tug of war or fetch, they would become too distracted and excited to focus on the principle of what you are attempting to teach them. With the help of the clicker, your dog will know what action they are doing correctly and what they are not, as the reward offers a bridging gap in time between the moment you want to reward your dog and the time the reward arrives. In a nutshell, the clicker teaches your dog how to become obedient and disciplined with the help of a mark that signals them to respond appropriately. Whatever you may use as your marker, whether it's the clicker or something else, you need to ensure that your dog only gets used to one sound or signal to prevent confusion.

The incredible thing about a clicker is that dogs who get trained with it to fix behavioral issues also love to learn with it in many other ways. You can teach your dog how to jump through a hoop with help from a clicker. Any type of positive reinforcement training, by using the clicker, can boost communication between you and your furry friend, strengthen your bond, and make training enjoyable for your dog. Keep in mind that some dogs are more intelligent than others, and the smarter your dog breed is, the more it will benefit from clicker training. It can stimulate dogs that are very intelligent by keeping them happy and healthy as a result of attention and learning.

Clicker training helps aggressive dogs by:

- Modifying behaviors, such as training your dog to remain calm. This is very difficult to accomplish with an aggressive puppy due to anxiety that causes aggressive behavior.
- Instilling another type of communication that is more likely to work because it is a new form of communication, compared to disciplining your puppy physically or ignoring, which can negatively affect your bond.
- Avoiding conflict by providing a hands-off approach, which is much better than getting physical with your puppy when they are aggressive or anxious.
- Promoting self-awareness in puppies to be aware of their behavior and to distinguish between right and wrong.
- Providing a source of entertainment for dogs, which has a positive effect on them and reduces their chances of becoming aggressive as a result of stress or anxiety.

- Feeling in control of something is important for a dog, especially for more intelligent breeds. Since they get something out of being good, they will respond better instead of aggressive.
- Reducing stress in your dog because you are using a contactless discipline method instead of becoming physical with your dog, which may cause it to be anxious and feel uncomfortable, and become more aggressive.
- Encouraging your dog to train and want to be disciplined because it helps them bond with their owner. Aggressive dogs generally don't have a good bond with their owner.
- Teaching your dog various behaviors, which helps them manage aggression or any other type of bad behavior safely or constructively.
- The training type is predictive and has the same outcome all the time, which is satisfying for your dog's mental health.

All of these effects that your puppy may experience, won't help them become an obedient dog or help with aggression problems. When you implement this type of training you don't have to worry about spending an entire day practicing it either. You simply need to get your puppy into the habit of clicker training, which can be done by implementing it a few times a day. With it, you can prevent them from showing any aggressive behavior that improves even more over time. Another dealbreaker for dogs is that they pick up on people's moods too, preferably their owner's mood, which they also respond to accordingly. So, if you remain calm, no matter how impatient you feel with your dog, you will provide them the space to learn effectively. The goal of clicker training is to keep your dog relaxed instead of scared or anxious. That's also why it's not a good idea to become physical with your dog. Many dog owners get this part of behavioral training wrong when they choose to discipline their dog physically instead of training properly.

If you get physical with your dog, you are teaching it to become even more aggressive and undisciplined, which is not the way you want to go, especially not with bigger dog breeds.

54

This may sound cliché, but your dog wants to make you happy, so if your mood is steady, your dog will meet you halfway. Since clicker training only involves good behavior from your dog, it also requires a positive and motivating mood from you. If you are not in a good mood, your dog will notice and have a more difficult time learning what they need to.

A good example of a lack of training in dogs with aggressive tendencies towards other dogs from a young age, include growling, biting, barking, and lunging towards other dogs they come into contact with. Clicker training is specifically successful in younger dogs. If you have an older dog that needs behavioral training, you may want to consider taking the dog to a professional trainer to have them assessed before you try addressing any behavioral problems yourself. When a trainer tries to teach a dog something, he or she will stimulate your dog's brain before they proceed with the lesson. This is done to put your dog in a more relaxed state of mind to ensure that they don't act aggressively towards the trainer, which will be a stranger at first to them.

A trainer will typically start with a treat and continue to give your dog treats with the help of a clicker to help your dog make the association between discipline and food rewards. After the initial training session, your trainer can advise you on how to proceed going forward. When you give your dog a treat, it is always recommended to praise your dog for what they have done right. Again, since your dog only wants to please you, its owner, it will remember the positive association.

Clicker training should be about ten minutes per session. The shorter the session, the more it will benefit your dog. A session longer than ten minutes may result in boredom and failure to pay attention to the training. Although it's recommended to implement clicker training every day, you can also, after a few weeks, start to implement it every two days or during different times each day. Since your dog doesn't generally get a lot of treats, they will be eager to please you to get it, which is the secret ingredient that makes clicker training so effective.

BEHAVIORAL THINGS TO KEEP IN MIND

1. Lack of mental stimulation

   Dogs that aren't mentally stimulated usually struggle with behavioral issues, no matter how big or small they are. Like humans need mental exercise, your dog needs it too because they also experience boredom and can become depressed if they don't receive the right amount of attention they need. Lack of mental stimulation is common in dogs with owners that don't understand or pay attention to what their pet needs. That's why it's significant to be aware of the attention a dog needs before you decide to get one. It may feel like your dog is doing fine on its own or can be left alone with a bowl of food and water for an entire day, but that is not always the case.

   Of course, people leave their dogs at home when they go to work or live their lives, but you should still give them enough attention and engage in activities to ensure they remain mentally strong. Something as little and simple as making your dog work by finding their meal or asking them to find a toy are simple things you can do every day to keep your fur-baby happy.

2. Health issues

   If your dog doesn't feel well physically or has an existing illness or injury, they can respond by misbehaving or becoming aggressive towards other dogs and people. When a dog acts out, it's easy to overlook this behavior as just being naughty or seeking attention, but it can be due to other problems. Should your dog feel unwell, they are more likely to show signs of a low mood. It is essential to not overlook bad behavior for this reason. If your dog is behaving particularly worse than normal for a prolonged period, it might be a good idea to take them to the vet for a check-up. Health issues that cause bad behavior can include arthritis, thyroid problems, sore teeth, hip dysplasia, luxating patellas, seizures, digestive issues, environmental or skin allergies, and ear infections. Hearing or eyesight loss and cancer can also be prime causes of bad dog behavior.

3. Bad genetics

    Behavioral issues can occur as a result of genetics. The most common behaviors include aggression and hyperactivity. So when you are taking in a dog, check whether you can find information about their parentage and whether they had positive temperaments. If they don't, your dog is likely to act out as they did and you will have no idea why. Even in this case, you can address bad behavior caused by poor genetics by placing your dog in a socialization program. The younger the dog is when you try to address this issue, the better the chances of the behavior correcting itself.

4. Lack of exercise

    Leaving your dog alone to run in a confined space or yard isn't exactly considered proper exercise. If you think of yourself in your office space or home kitchen, you can't exercise in these places, can you? Well, neither can your dog. Just like you need a wide-open space to exercise, so does your puppy, which is why taking it for a walk at least once a day for fifteen minutes is the most ideal option. This will keep your dog healthy, happy, and relaxed, which will prevent stress and anxiety, which generally causes bad behavior. You can also play games with your dog in a park or a field by playing catch or chasing them around.

5. Inconsistent environment

If you allow your dog to jump on you sometimes, but not all the time, it's not sending them the right message, is it? You are telling your dog that it's okay to jump on you when you allow them, and then confuses them when you don't. Dogs need to get used to patterns. If a dog has two owners and is taught differently by both owners, the dog won't understand what it can and can't do. When learning patterns are confusing to them, they become anxious, which also results in them acting out. The same goes for when you confuse your dog and scold them for something you once encouraged.

When your dog jumps on you, and you want to break this pattern, you can ignore the action to reinforce the behavior you want from your dog. You should not react negatively or scold your dog when they jump on you, bark, or do something bad. Instead, you should ignore them, because if you respond to your dog, they will think you are giving them attention as a result of their action and will do it again. It's necessary to have consistent boundaries and rules in the house when you have a dog. Everyone in your house should also understand and implement these rules for your dog to truly grasp them.

6. Misunderstanding correct behavior

Just because a dog barks, jumps up to greet, pulls on the leash, guards their food, growls when threatened, or chews on everything, doesn't mean that they behave badly. That's just regular dog behavior you signed up for when you decided to get a puppy. The extent of a dog's 'behavior' depends on the breed. If you are considering a German Shepard, expect a dog that barks often and loudly. When you take in a Siberian Husky, you can expect a dog that digs holes, is regularly hyperactive and cries or howls about almost everything. With a golden retriever, you can expect less bad behavior compared to a German Shepherd or Husky. Some smaller dogs are easier to control, depending on their breed, but they can also be a handful. That's why it's so important to teach your dog how to behave the way you want them to. If your puppy does something you don't like, teach them what not to do with the help of a clicker, but don't think regular dog behavior is bad behavior. You aren't dealing with a toy, a dog is a living breathing animal that needs guidance.

7. Diet changes

    You may have heard that you should keep your dog's diet the same, except for when you have to change your puppy's food to adult food once they've reached that stage. The same goes for when they reached the senior phase of life. You should also check the quality of dog food. Some cheap brands do not contain the nutritional content that your dog needs to stay healthy. The older your dog gets, the more expensive dog food will get, especially with senior dogs who need specialized and nutrient-formulated food to keep health in check.

    When you feed your dog a high-quality food diet, they will be on their best behavior. If a dog needs to transition to a new type of food, it may take some time to adapt.

8. Routine changes

    Dogs require security to remain calm, and the more stressed out your dog is, the more they misbehave. That is why they need to stick to a solid routine, which includes feeding them at the same time, going for walks, regular bathing, and playtime on schedule. Once you have a routine set in place, your dog will have less anxiety. If you let your dog sleep inside of your house and then suddenly keep it outside at night, expect a negative response. In this case, you may find them barking more or acting out with you and other dogs.

    As you can imagine, when a new pet or baby joins your household, your dog will also be confused because their routine will be affected. In either of these cases, you should make sure to keep your dog in the same routine as much you can to prevent them from feeling left out, neglected, or become aggressive.

9. The presence of fear periods

    The trick to good behavior is to take your puppy out of any state of fear they may have. If you have a generally fearless dog that acts in the opposite way, remember that a puppy's brain also undergoes development. It's normal for puppies to experience periods of fear, especially during the first 8 to 12 weeks of life, or the first 5 to 6 months. The duration of the period where your dog may experience fear depends on the breed.

    If you are worried about your puppy, it's good to wait a week or two before taking them to the vet or a training class, or even a groomer. If anything frightens your dog, this is a critical time for you to make them understand that you are there as a means of comfort and to provide safety. This will cause your dog to rely on you whenever something goes wrong and strengthen your bond, which can also help dogs have an easier time complying with what you need from them.

10. Negative or lack of socialization

    It's important to provide your puppy with exposure to other dogs to get used to them and learn how to behave around them. Socialization with other dogs, however, needs to be controlled. Your puppy also has to get used to many different sounds, people, surfaces, and experiences, if they are going to understand how to adopt the right behavior in different settings. With clicker training, it's necessary to train your dog in different settings and around various people and dogs to make them used to your demands without them being compromised in another environment. Placing your dog in a puppy class can be a good and fun way to get your dog used to other dogs and build socialization skills.

    Although socialization from a young age can help your dog, they can still develop negative behaviors, particularly when attacked, teased, or scolded by other dogs or people. Bad experiences at the vet, groomer, and training classes can also play a role in your dog's negative behavior. Keeping your dog away from other people, dogs, or even alone for too long will have the same bad effect long-term. This is also a mistake many dog owners make.

11. Inappropriate elimination

Your puppy doesn't understand when it does right or wrong, so you have to teach it. You can't make them sleep outside because they did something bad or keep toys, treats, or exercise away because of behavior. This is not a positive reinforcement, which is ideally what you want to focus on when you train your dog. Instead of taking something away and causing them more anxiety and stress, focus on clicker training to help them understand the difference between right and wrong by making positive associations for your dog.

HOW TO CORRECT BAD BEHAVIOR
Barking

Causes: Vocalization, such as barking, howling, or whining occurs with the purpose to warn or alert, seek attention, anxiety, boredom, playfulness or excitement, and as a response to other dogs.

Solution: You can learn how to control barking by teaching your dog bark and quiet commands. This requires you to be patient and consistent with training and can be done with the help of a clicker. Once you understand why your dog is barking, whether it's a normal response or a behavioral issue, you can treat it accordingly. With a clicker, you can approach your dog every time they bark excessively. You should then tell your dog to sit and stop barking, click the clicker once they have stopped, and present a treat.

Chewing

Causes: Teething, anxiety, curiosity, boredom, or a lack of exercise that results in too much-stored energy.

Solution: You can encourage your pet to chew on specific things that are allowed like designated dog-friendly chew toys. Try to keep all personal things away from your puppy, and when you are not present, confine your dog so that they are not tempted to act out. If you catch them chewing on something they shouldn't, distract your dog with a loud noise, replace the chew toy and ensure your dog gets a lot of exercises and mental stimulation to avoid the same behavior.

Jumping up

Causes: Excitement, anxiety, and seeking items or food out of your hands.

Solution: Turn away from your dog or ignore them completely. Don't scold your dog. If it is necessary, walk away without making eye contact, touching, or speaking to them. The dog may continue to jump on you or try to get your attention, but will eventually stop because they expect a reaction from you. Once they stop, continue ignoring your dog until their attention is switched to something else.

Separation anxiety

Causes: Behavioral problems brought on by anxiety when you leave the house, your dog follows you around constantly, misbehavior occurs once you leave the house, and your dog tries to come into contact with you at all times.

Solution: Proper training and extra attention to your pet is required to solve separation anxiety. This involves behavior modification and can be accomplished with the help of desensitization exercises. In extreme cases, your dog's vet will also prescribe medication to keep them from experiencing high levels of anxiety.

Digging

Causes: Boredom, hunting instinct, fear, anxiety, comfort-seeking, the desire to hide things, or wanting to escape.

Solution: Digging can be brought on by disruptive tendencies to misbehave, which is why you need to ensure your dog is getting enough exercise. If they continue to dig holes in the yard, be sure to train harder and spend more time on this. If your dog still can't stop digging, give them a sandbox to dig in as a game, but train them to only use the sandbox to dig holes and not your yard.

Messing indoors or publicly

Causes: Territorial marking, lack of adequate housebreaking training, excitement urination, and anxiety.

Solution: In puppies, inappropriate elimination can't be helped as your dog doesn't know any better, especially not before 12 weeks old. After your puppy has reached 12 weeks, however, you can train them to not mess indoors. If you have an older dog, you need to check with your vet whether your dog has any health issues. If not, then you can consult a dog trainer to teach your dog correctly.

Begging

Causes: A habit that does not get rectified with training or scolding your dog because they are begging, which causes excitement and makes your dog want to do it again.

Solution: Before making food or eating, tell your dog to go lie down where they are not able to stare at you. This can be done by confining your dog in a different room. If they behave, you can give them a treat after you and your household have finished eating.

Chasing

Causes: Behavioral issues brought on by keeping your dog on a leash or confined too much when you are outdoors, not training your dog to come to you when you alert them, and excitement triggers like other dogs or joggers.

Solution: Discover why your dog chases by remaining aware of their behavior outdoors. When your dog chases another animal or person, keep it from getting out of control by doing what you can to get your dog on a leash again. Dedicated training with a clicker can help you keep your dog focused and prevent it from running off.

Biting

Causes: Predatory instinct, sickness or being in physical pain, protective tendencies, fear, and defensiveness.

Solution: Figure out why your dog bites by first eliminating the option that they could be sick or in pain by taking your dog to the vet for a check-up. If a dog is healthy but continues to bite other dogs or people, you must provide them with proper training, breeding practices, and socialization with other dogs and people from a young age to correct the behavior. If your dog is out of control or at an adult stage, you can consult a dog trainer for help.

CONCLUSION

We have come to the end of this book, and I truly want to thank you for buying it, as well as congratulate you for reading it to the very end. The fact that you made it here is a clear sign you have a real desire to improve at training your dog using positive reinforcement.

It is my hope that after reading this far, you now have a solid foundation and are ready to take your puppy to the next level. The purpose of this book was to show you the right approach to take when you decide to start training your pet with the help of a clicker.

After realizing that many people around the world face the same common problems when they first begin clicker training, I decided it was time to address those issues and create something that would make your journey faster, smoother, and more rewarding.

Remember, consistency is the key to success, and without it, you won't get very far. Have patience with your puppy or adult dog, and believe me, results will start to show.

Now it's up to you to put into practice the information this book provides, and to build lasting, positive habits in your dog. Take action today, and tomorrow will be better than today, not only for you, but for your dog as well.

REFERENCES

February 16, D., & Pm, 2015 at 12:14. (n.d.). *Clicker Training*. Positively.com. https://positively.com/dog-training/methods-equipment/training-methods/clicker-training/

Fulcher, Sarah., (2017, May 1). *Ten Reasons Your Dog May Develop Behavior Problems | Karen Pryor Clicker Training*. (2014, January 2). Www.Clickertraining.com. https://www.clickertraining.com/ten-reasons-your-dog-may-develop-behavior-problems

Gibeault, Stephanie., MSc, Dec 24, C., Dec 24, 2019 | 4 Minutes, & Minutes, 2019 | 4. (2019, December 24). *Clicker Training: Learn About Mark & Reward Dog Training Using Clickers*. American Kennel Club. https://www.akc.org/expert-advice/training/clicker-training-your-dog-mark-and-reward/

Pryor, Karen., (2012, January 9). *The Eight Ways of Changing Behavior | Karen Pryor Clicker Training*. (2012, September 5). Www.Clickertraining.com. https://www.clickertraining.com/node/290

Stregowski, Jenna., (2019, August 31). *How to Solve 10 of the Biggest Dog Behavior Problems*. The Spruce Pets. https://www.thesprucepets.com/common-dog-behavior-problems-1118278

Valitutti, C., (2020, June 23). *Does Clicker Training Work For Aggressive Dogs?* Dog House Times. https://doghousetimes.com/clickers-and-aggressive-dogs/

www.ingramcontent.com/pod-product-compliance
Lightning Source LLC
Chambersburg PA
CBHW061318120626
46546CB00007B/2637